SALTASAURUS

by Janet Riehecky
illustrated by Betty Raskin

THE
CHILD'S
WORLD

MANKATO, MN

*Grateful appreciation is expressed to
Bret S. Beall, Research Consultant,
Field Museum of Natural History, Chicago,
Illinois, who reviewed this book to
insure its accuracy.*

Library of Congress Cataloging in Publication Data

Riehecky, Janet, 1953-
    Saltasaurus / by Janet Riehecky; illustrated by Betty Raskin.
        p. cm. — (Dinosaur books)
    Summary: Presents facts and speculations about the physical
characteristics and behavior of this armored dinosaur.
    ISBN 0-89565-635-3 (lib. bdg.)
    1. Saltasaurus—Juvenile literature.   [1. Saltasaurus.
2. Dinosaurs.]   I. Raskin, Betty, 1953-   ill.   II. Title.   III. Series:
Riehecky, Janet, 1953-   Dinosaur books.
QE862.S3R538   1990
567.9'7—dc20
                                                    90-2473
                                                      CIP
                                                       AC

SALTASAURUS

Two kinds of dinosaurs roamed the earth millions of years ago. There were plant eaters who ate leaves, pine needles, or twigs. And there were meat eaters . . .

who ate the plant eaters! Plant-eating
dinosaurs did whatever they could to keep
the meat eaters away.

Some plant eaters found protection in their size. They grew so huge that only a really hungry meat eater would even think of bothering them.

Some plant eaters used weapons for protection. Some had whiplike tails which they could use to knock meat eaters down or even break their legs.

Others had claws to use as weapons.
They could slash at meat eaters, fighting
fiercely to defend themselves.

Others did not need to fight. Their armor protected them from the meat eaters' sharp teeth.

One type of dinosaur didn't take any chances. It used *all* these methods to protect itself. This dinosaur was the Saltasaurus (salt-uh-SAWR-us), named for the place where it was found, the province of Salta in Argentina.

The Saltasaurus grew to a huge size. It was about forty feet in length and weighed about thirty tons. That's almost the size of a small house!

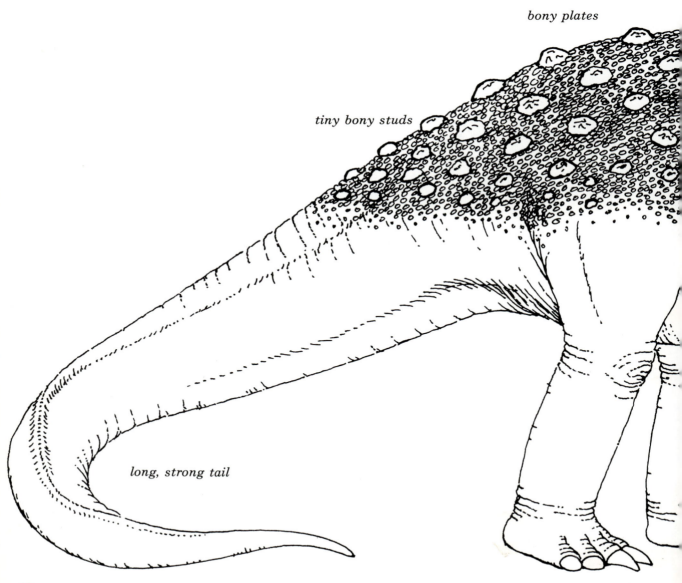

bony plates

tiny bony studs

long, strong tail

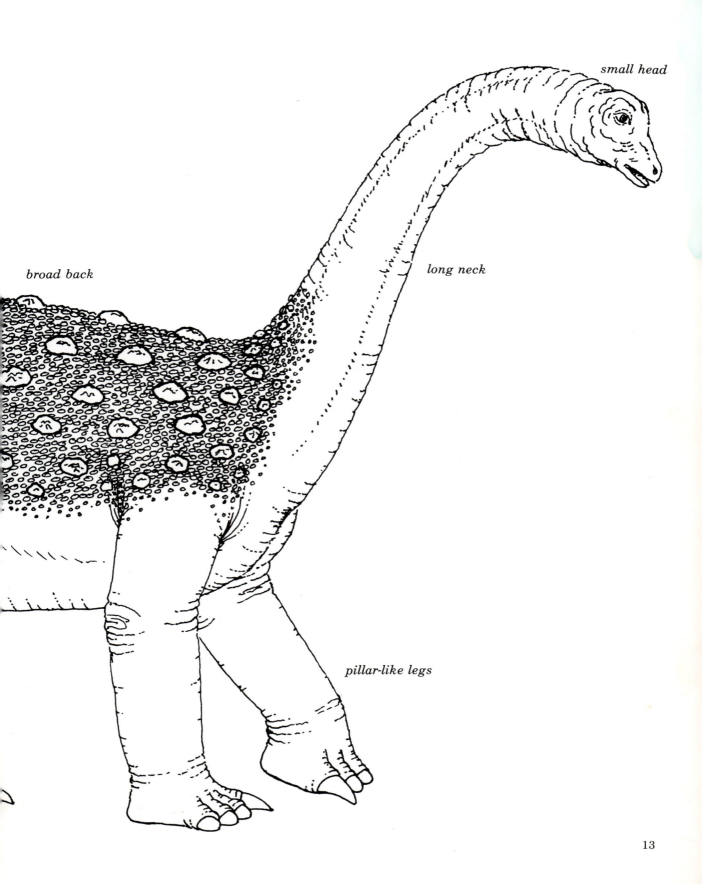

small head

broad back

long neck

pillar-like legs

The long, thick tail of the Saltasaurus made a great weapon. It could bend easily in many directions to strike at an attacker.

On each front foot the Saltasaurus had a
large, sharp claw. It could rear up on its
back legs, keeping its balance with its tail,
and slash at a hungry meat eater.

In addition to the Saltasaurus' size, tail, and claws, it had an almost fool-proof defense: armor. Bony plates and bumps were spread across its back, neck and tail.

The bony plates on the Saltasaurus were about two to four inches wide and were scattered across the creature's skin. Between the plates were tiny lumps of bone, thousands of them, protecting the dinosaur from teeth and claws.

This coat of armor made it very hard for any meat eater to have a Saltasaurus snack.

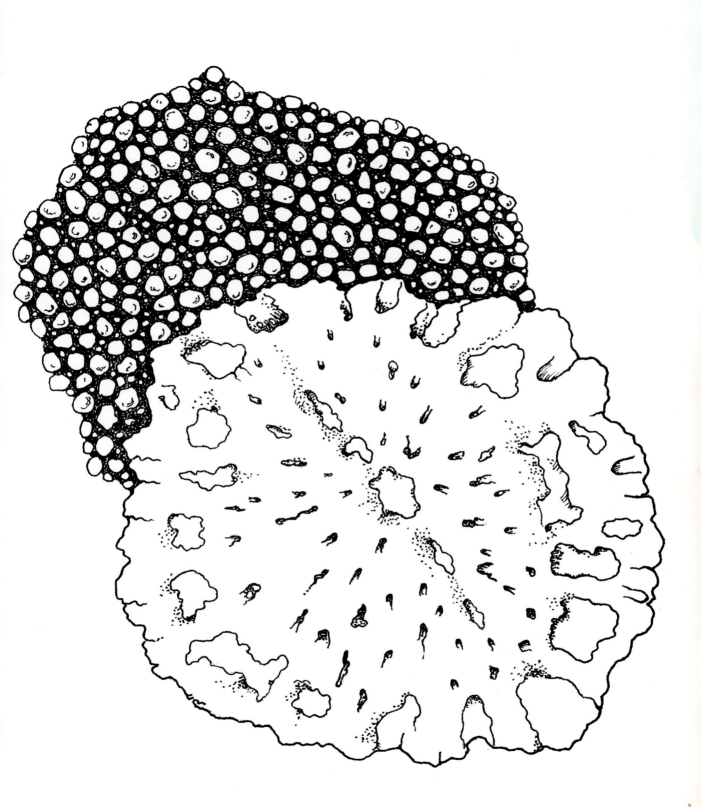

19

Scientists think the Saltasaurus lived a life similar to the other really big plant eaters. It probably spent most of its time eating—and eating and eating. A creature that large would have needed to eat almost constantly.

Scientists think the Saltasaurus ate everything in sight. They think it could rear up on its back legs to reach leaves and pine needles high above the ground. It probably stripped each branch, swallowed without chewing, and went on to the next branch.

The stomach of the Saltasaurus had to work very hard to digest all those plants. But the Saltasaurus tried to give it some help. Scientists think it ate a few rocks now and then. The rocks, bouncing around in its stomach, helped the Saltasaurus digest its food by breaking the plants into smaller pieces.

Scientists learn about dinosaurs' eating habits by studying fossils. They have not found very many fossils of the Saltasaurus, but they think it was like the other really big dinosaurs.

Scientists have found footprints and tail prints of big dinosaurs. These prints show that the dinosaurs reared up on their back legs, using their tails as props. Scientists think the Saltasaurus did that too.

The teeth and jaws of all the big dinosaurs show that they ate plants and that they probably couldn't chew their food. And when scientists find smooth stones with a special kind of shiny covering near a dinosaur's stomach, they know that those stones were in the dinosaur's stomach.

Scientists don't agree about how big dinosaurs, such as the Saltasaurus, had babies. Some scientists suggest they had their babies alive. That's because they have a hard time imagining how a huge dinosaur could lay eggs without crushing them. Others suggest the Saltasaurus laid eggs in long straight lines to keep from stepping on them. (One dinosaur's eggs were found like that.) But many scientists think they just made a simple nest—and were very careful where they put their feet.

Scientists also aren't sure whether dinosaurs like the Saltasaurus took care of
their babies after they were born. Some
scientists think big dinosaurs weren't
smart enough to be good parents. But
they do think that young dinosaurs were

welcomed into a herd when they grew big enough to keep up. The littler Saltasaurs would have stayed in the middle with the larger ones forming a wall of protection around them.

However the Saltasaurus lived, it must have been a good life. The Saltasaurus lived until the end of the age of dinosaurs. Most of the other really big dinosaurs became extinct millions of years before that.

The Saltasaurus was successful at gathering food and defending itself from meat eaters, but in the end that wasn't enough. It became extinct sixty-five million years ago—along with all the other dinosaurs.

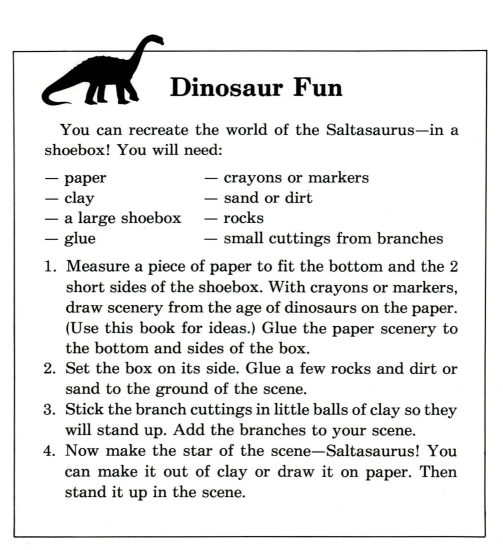

Dinosaur Fun

You can recreate the world of the Saltasaurus—in a shoebox! You will need:

— paper   — crayons or markers
— clay   — sand or dirt
— a large shoebox — rocks
— glue   — small cuttings from branches

1. Measure a piece of paper to fit the bottom and the 2 short sides of the shoebox. With crayons or markers, draw scenery from the age of dinosaurs on the paper. (Use this book for ideas.) Glue the paper scenery to the bottom and sides of the box.
2. Set the box on its side. Glue a few rocks and dirt or sand to the ground of the scene.
3. Stick the branch cuttings in little balls of clay so they will stand up. Add the branches to your scene.
4. Now make the star of the scene—Saltasaurus! You can make it out of clay or draw it on paper. Then stand it up in the scene.